Animal Cracker Uppers

SUPER
FUNNY
ANIMAL JOKES

RICHARD LEDERER & JIM ERTNER

International Punsters of the Year

ILLUSTRATIONS BY JIM MCLEAN

Marion Street Press

Portland, Oregon

To my wife, Ruth, who has always encouraged me to write joke books for kids. —Jim Ertner

To my punderful grandchildren—Maud, Mattias, Leo, Lucy, and Nelly. —Richard Lederer

Published by Marion Street Press
4207 SE Woodstock Blvd # 168
Portland, OR 97206-6267
USA
http://www.marionstreetpress.com

Orders and review copies: 800-888-4741

Printed in the United States of America
ISBN 978-1-933338-88-0

Copyedited by Lorna Gusner

Library of Congress Cataloging-in-Publication Data

Lederer, Richard, 1938-
   Super funny animal jokes / Richard Lederer and Jim Ertner, international punsters of the year ; illustrated by Jim McLean.
      p. cm. -- (Animal cracker uppers)
   ISBN 978-1-933338-88-0 (pbk.)
   1. Animals--Juvenile humor. I. Ertner, James D. II. McLean, Jim, 1928- III. Title.
   PN6231.A5L448 2011
   818'.5402--dc22

2011005348

CONTENTS

PART 2
Even More Animal Jokes

INTRODUCTION

Animals
    run and gallop,
        hop and jump,
            fly and soar,
                and swim and dive
through our everyday lives.

Animals live in our language:
    "blind as a bat,"
        "happy as a clam (or lark),"
            "stubborn as a mule,"
                "crazy as a bedbug (or loon),"
                    and "wise as an owl."

Animals become symbols of athletic excellence:
    the Chicago Bears,
        the Atlanta Falcons,
            the Arizona Diamondbacks,
                the Toronto Raptors,
                  and the San Jose Sharks.

And everybody loves animal jokes:
    Duck jokes quack you up.
    Porcupine jokes are sharp and to-the-point.
    Sponge jokes are absorbing.
    Elephant jokes are worth the weight.
    Skunk jokes are real stinkers, but they become
    best-smellers.

Here are more than 500 animal jokes that are guaranteed to make you

       howl,

              twitter,

                        yip,

                                 and yelp

with lots of laughter.

PART 1
A DICTIONARY
OF ANIMAL JOKES

Aardvark

Aardvark: Aan aanimal that resembles the aanteater.

Alligator

What do you call a creature that has huge jaws, a tail, and lives in dark places between buildings?

An alleygator.

What kind of alligators steer ships and boats?

Navigators.

Amoeba

An amoeba is a mathematically inclined organism that multiplies by dividing.

How do amoebas call home?

On their single-cell phones.

Animals (in general)

What did the spelling teacher say to the gorilla?

"U R N N M L."

Holiday greeting sign at an animal shelter: We Fish Ewe A Furry Meowy Christmas Panda Hippo Gnu Deer.

Ant

What do ants say to each other?

They just make small talk.

Cheerios are hula-hoops for ants.

Speaking of cereal, why did the ant race across the top of a cereal box?

Because the directions on the box read, "Tear along the dotted line."

What happened when the Pink Panther stepped on an insect?"

[singing] "Dead-ant. Dead-ant. Dead-ant, dead-ant, dead-ant . . ."

There once was a fellow from France
Whose hobby was searching for ants,
Till he took quite a spill
In a tiny red hill
And wound up with ants in his pants.

Ape

Who is the world's biggest monarch?
King Kong.

Why did King Kong climb up the Empire State Building?
He was too big to fit in an elevator.

What did Judy Garland sing to a big ape?
"King Kong, the witch is dead."

What did King Kong say to the pilots who attacked him?
"Excuse me. I have to catch a plane."

Did you hear about the gorilla that invented a bell that would ring whenever somebody scored in table tennis?
It was called the King Kong Ping Pong Ding Dong.

As King Kong said after meeting Godzilla, "Small world, isn't it?"

Baboon

Who was the famous French monkey general?
Ape-oleon Baboon-aparte.

Bat

Why do bats hang upside down?
So they can drop off to sleep.

Bats are fly-by-night operators.

Bear

What do you call a naked grizzly?
> *A bare bear.*

> *Fuzzy Wuzzy was a bear.*
> *Fuzzy Wuzzy had no hair.*
> *Fuzzy Wuzzy wasn't very fuzzy, was he?*

What do you call a grizzly that likes to sunbathe?
> *A solar bear.*

Did you hear about the two dumb guys who went to see the bears at Yellowstone National Park?
> *When they saw a sign that read "BEAR LEFT," they went home.*

Beaver

What did the beaver say to the tree?
> *"It's been nice gnawing you."*

Bee

Why is the letter A like a flower?
> *Because a B always comes after it.*

Did you hear about the worker bees that went on strike?
> *They wanted more honey and shorter flowers.*

What do bees do with their honey?
> *They cell it.*

What is the healthiest insect?
A vitamin bee one.

> *There was a man who loved the bees.*
> *He always was their friend.*
> *He liked to sit upon their hives,*
> *But they stung him in the end.*

Did you hear about the beekeeper who processed honey in a blender and whipped it into a foamy fountain of sticky sweetness?

> *He videotaped the process and sent it to the TV show "America's Honeyest Foam Videos."*

What do insects take when they're ill?
Antibeeotics.

Bird

Why do birds fly south for the winter?
It's too far to walk.

Why are birds grouchy in the morning?
Their bills are over dew.

What do you call a bath in cold water?
A brrrrrd bath.

What do you call a wizard who moves through the air like a bird?
A flying sorcerer.

Bison

What did the buffalo say to his boy when he departed on a long journey?

"Bison."

Bloodhound

What's Dracula's favorite breed of dog?

Bloodhound.

Boa

Did you hear about the two boa constrictors that got married?

They had a crush on each other.

What did the pet store owner name his boa constrictor?

Julius Squeezer.

Bug

Did you hear about the entomologist?

His job drove him buggy.

Did you hear about the female bedbug?

She had a baby in the spring.

Burro

Why was it difficult making a living in the Old West?

Because people had to beg, burro, and steal.

Butterfly

A butterfly will flutter by.

Camel

A camel is a horse that swallowed its saddle.

What do you call a camel with one hump? *A dromedary.*

And a camel with two humps? *A bactrian.*

And what do you call a camel with no humps? *Humphrey.*

Canary

What did the 500-pound canary say as it walked down the street?

"Here kitty, kitty!"

What do you call a canary run over by a lawnmower?
Shredded tweet.

What do you call a canary that flies into a pastry dish?
Tweetie Pie.

Carp

How do fish travel to work?
In carp pools.

Cat

Did you hear about the guy whose cat got run over by a steamroller?
He just stood there with a long puss.

A cat stole a ball of yarn, but the mystery was soon unraveled.

Where might you find a psychic cat?
At the E.S.P.C.A.

What is the worst weather for mice?
When it's raining cats and dogs.

What's even worse than raining cats and dogs?
Hailing taxicabs.

Caterpillar

A caterpillar is an upholstered worm.

Did you hear about the caterpillar's New Year's resolution?
It promised to turn over a new leaf.

Catfish

Why did the boy bait his hook with a dead mouse?
He was fishing for catfish.

Cattle

What two members of the cow family go everywhere with you?
Your calves.

What key do cattle sing in?
Beef-flat.

What happens to a cow when it gives birth?
It gets de-calf-inated.

What do you call a cow with two legs?
Lean beef.

What do you call a cow with no legs?
Ground beef.

What else do you call a cow with no legs?
It doesn't matter what you call him. He still won't come.

Centipede

Teacher: "Why were you late to school this morning?"
Centipede student: "It took me an hour to put on my galoshes."

A centipede was happy quite, until a frog in fun
Said, "Pray, which leg comes after which?"
This raised her mind to such a pitch,
She lay distracted in a ditch
Considering how to run.

What has a hundred legs and goes, "Ho ho ho!"?
A Santapede.

I'm as unhappy as a tender-footed centipede on a hot pavement.

Chameleon

Did you hear about the lizard that tells jokes and changes colors?
It's a stand-up chameleon.

Cheetah

Why is it dangerous to play poker in the jungle?
Because of all the lion cheetahs.

Chicken

What do you call a hen that gets sunburned in Florida?
Southern fried chicken.

Why did the chicken cross the road?
To get away from Colonel Sanders.

What did the hen do when it saw a large order of Kentucky Fried Chicken?

> *It kicked the bucket.*

Did you hear about the new cookbook entitled "How to Fry Chicken"?

> *It's by Ken Tucky.*

What do you call a cowardly skin diver?

> *Chicken of the Sea.*

Why did the man always order Chicken Napoleon?

> *So he could pull the bone apart.*

Chihuahua

A man was out walking his little dog and decided that he wanted to eat in a fancy restaurant. So he put on dark glasses and entered the restaurant with his dog. The maître d' explained to the man that restaurants do not allow pets and that he could not enter the place with his dog.

"But I'm blind, and this animal is my seeing-eye dog," the man explained.

"But you're walking with a Chihuahua," said the maître d'.

"What? A Chihuahua!" exclaimed the man. "You mean they gave me a Chihuahua?"

Chimpanzee

Did you hear about the baby monkey?

> *He was a chimp off the old block.*

Why was Tarzan so hard to get along with?
He had a chimp on his shoulder.

Clam

What is stranger than seeing a shrimp roll?
Seeing a clam bake.

Cockatoo

Did you hear about the arrogant parrot?
It was a cocky-too.

Cockroach

Did you hear about the cockroach doll?
You wind it up and it runs under the kitchen sink.

Cod

What lives at the bottom of the ocean and makes you an offer you can't refuse?
The Codfather.

What is the fiercest fish in the ocean?
Codzilla.

Crab

Why does the ocean roar?
You'd roar too if you had crabs on your bottom.

Why was the crab arrested?
He was always pinching things.

Crocodile

Girl: "I've got a crocodile named Ginger."

Boy: "Does Ginger bite?"

Girl: "No, but Ginger snaps."

The prosecutor confronted the criminal crocodile and asked if he killed the man in cold blood. The crocodile replied, "Of course I did it in cold blood. I'm a reptile."

Crow

Sign in pet store: Caw us and we'll tweet you right.

Why did the crow run up a huge phone bill?
　　She made too many long-distance caws.

Dachshund

Why did the cowboy buy a dachshund?

Because his favorite song was "Get Along Little Doggie."

What advice should be given to small canines who can't find a fire hydrant or a tree?

"Get a lawn, little doggie."

Dalmatian

Why do Dalmatians have a hard time hiding?
Because they're always spotted.

Deer

Why was the doe playing in the storm?
Because it was a rain-deer.

What do you call someone who becomes a deer whenever there's a full moon?
A weirdoe.

What do you call a deer that can kick a ball with his left and right feet?
Bambidextrous

Dinosaur

A dinosaur is a colossal fossil.

How did the student dinosaur pass his exams?
With extinction.

What did the cavewoman say to her husband while they were surrounded by a herd of dinosaurs?
"Don't just stand there. Slay something."

Who saw the Tyrannosaurus come into the restaurant?
The diners saw.

Why don't they include dinosaurs in animal crackers?
Because they're extinct, and they'd be too big to fit in the box.

Doe

What food do deer like the best?
Doe-nuts.

What deer are extinct?
Doe does.

Dog

We hope we don't sound doggone dogmatic when we say, "Hot dog! It's time that you make these pages dog-eared."

Why was the dog summoned to appear in court?
Because it got a barking ticket.

What did the owner say to his dog, after giving him a special treat?
"Bone appetit."

Doctor: "Walking your dog is good for weight loss."

Patient: "Yes, but who wants a skinny dog?"

Did you hear about the dog who chased cars?
He ended up exhausted.

Why did the dog have a flat nose?
From chasing parked cars.

Why did the man name his dogs Timex and Rolex?
Because they're watchdogs.

Donkey

What keys won't open doors?
Donkeys (as well as monkeys and turkeys).

Dove

What has a shell and flies?
A turtle-dove.

Dragon

How do dragons vent their frustrations?
They let off steam.

A dragon came home from work and asked, "Am I late for dinner?"

"Yes," was the reply. "Everyone's eaten."

Duck

Why did the man use a duck as an alarm clock?
So it would wake him up at the quack of dawn.

What happens when a duck flies upside down?
It quacks up.

What bird is useful in boxing matches?
Duck.

The price of duck feathers has vastly increased. Now even down is up.

When it comes to ugly ducklings, it takes swan to know one.

Eagle

Did you hear about the man whose wife is like a bird?
She watches him like a hawk with eagle eyes.

Eel

What is an eel's favorite sport?
Ice shockey.

Where do young fish study and learn?
In eel-ementary schools.

Why do eels always know the latest news?
Because they keep up with current events.

Elephant

Why are there so many elephant jokes?
Because it's never hard to find a new wrinkle.

What should you do if a herd of elephants rushes toward you while you're in a telephone booth?
Make a collect call and reverse the charge.

Why do elephants have trunks?
They can't afford suitcases.

Two elephants, Harry and Fay,
Couldn't kiss with their trunks in the way.
So they boarded a plane,
They're now kissing in Maine,
'Cause their trunks got sent to L.A.

Why are elephants wrinkled?
Have you ever tried to iron one?

Who weighs 6,000 pounds and wears glass slippers?
Cinderelephant.

Ewe

A monk used to peddle flowers in front of an office building, but he really annoyed the tenants with his persistent sales tactics. The tenants finally bought a lamb and tied it up outside the building near the monk. The lamb's continual bleating drove the monk away. Which just goes to show that only ewes can prevent florist friars.

Fawn

What did the buck say to the doe?
"Let's have a little fawn, baby."

Firefly

Did you hear about the two fireflies that met at sunrise?
It was love at first light.

What did the frog have for a light meal?
A firefly.

Fish

Did you hear about the fisherwoman named Annette?
She really got caught up in her work.

Why can't you expect fishermen to be generous?
Because their business makes them sell fish.

Two members of a monastery decided to open a fish-and-chips eatery in order to make a little extra spending money. On opening day, the first customer complained to one of the new owners about his over-cooked filet of sole. (Soul food, of course, was the specialty of these men of the cloth.)
"I'm very sorry," said the co-owner, "but you'll have to speak with the fish friar. I'm just the chip monk."

What's the difference between a newspaper and a television set?
You can't wrap fish and chips in a television set.

What is a sea monster's favorite meal?
Fish and ships.

Flamingo

What fiery letter is like a flamingo?
A flaming "O."

Flea

Did you hear about the dog who went to a flea circus?
He stole the whole show.

As one flea said to another, "Shall we walk or take the dog?"

As the flea said to her husband, "Let's go out for a bite."

> *A flea and a fly in a flue*
> *Were imprisoned, so what could they do?*
> *Said the flea, "Let us fly!"*
> *Said the fly, "Let us flee!"*
> *So they flew through a flaw in the flue.*

Flounder

Did you hear about the new organization for fish?
It was formed by several flounders.

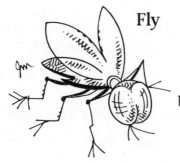

Fly

What kind of paper is best for making kites?
Flypaper.

> *Nothing makes one hotter*
> *Than wielding a fly swatter.*
> *But it's all we've got*
> *To teach those flies what's swat.*

Tourist: "Don't you ever shoo all these flies?"
Native: "No, we just let them go barefoot."

A mother fly complained after a sleepless night, "Junior was sick, and I had to walk the ceiling with him all night."

Foal

Did you hear about the horse that was born on the first day of the fourth month?

It was an April foal.

Frog

What is the name of the new science fantasy film epic in which the main characters are frogs?

Star Warts.

Did you hear about the man who swallowed a frog?

He's likely to croak any minute.

Did you hear about the cowardly frog?

She was a chicken croakette.

What is a frog's favorite snack?

French flies and a large Croak at the IHOP.

> *A princess who lived near a bog*
> *Met a prince in the form of a frog.*
> *Now she and her prince*
> *Are the parents of quints:*
> *Four girls and one polliwog.*

Giraffe

Did you hear about the giraffe race?
>*It was neck-and-neck all the way.*

Where do giraffes hang out?
>*At Giraffe-ic Park.*

What's tall and flowery?
>*A giraffodil.*

Did you hear about the student who decided to write an essay on a giraffe?

First he got a really big ladder.

Did you hear about the writing on a tall wall at the zoo?

It was giraffiti.

Gnat

Girl: "What's the difference between a gnat and a gnatterbaby?"

Mother: "What's a gnatterbaby?"

Girl: "Nothing. What's a gnatter with you?"

Gnu

What do antelopes read every morning at breakfast?

The daily gnuspaper.

Two lions were the leaders of their pride. While searching for their evening meal, they came upon two unsuspecting gnus and devoured them. "That," announced one of the kings of the jungle, "is the end of the gnus. And here, once again, are the head lions."

Goat

What is the world's best butter?

A goat.

Or, as the mother goat scolded her kid, "I don't want to hear another word. No ifs, no ands, and no butts."

Goldfish

As one goldfish said to another while swimming in a bowl, "See you around."

Goose

What is unique about a goose?
> *It's the only animal that grows down as it grows up.*

As the baby goose said when it heard a car honk in the night, "Is that you, ma?"

Gopher

What did the woman say when her figurine of a rodent crashed to the floor?
> *"Gopher broke."*

Gorilla

What do you call an 800-pound gorilla?
> *Sir.*

Why did the ape join the Marine Corps?
> *He wanted to learn about gorilla warfare.*

Grasshopper

A grasshopper is an insect on a pogo stick.

Greyhound

When is a black dog not a black dog?
> *When it's a greyhound.*

A greyhound trainer is a race cur driver.

Great Dane

Did you hear about the Great Dane that was purchased by an unsuspecting family?
> *He had the house broken before he was.*

Hare

Rabbit fur is hare hair.

Did you hear about the rich rabbit?
He was a million-hare.

What do you call a row of rabbits walking backward?
A receding hare line.

Heifer

A farmer once called his cow Zephyr,
She seemed such an amiable hephyr.
When the farmer drew near,
She kicked off his ear,
Which made him considerably dephyr.

Hen

Why did the hen sit on an axe?
So she could hatchet.

Woman No. 1: "If you think your hairdo is nice, wait until you see my hendo."
Woman No. 2: "What's a hendo?"
Woman No. 1: "It lays eggs."

What is a hen's favorite dessert?
Layer cake.

Why was the chicken farmer unhappy?
Because he was henpecked.

Why did the hen stop right in the middle of the road?
It was a for layin' highway, and she wanted to lay it on the line.

Hippopotamus

A hippopotamus went to the doctor and complained of a failing appetite: "I just peck at my food these days. A peck of this and a peck of that."

What weighs over a ton, feels cold to the touch, and comes on a stick?

A hippopopsicle.

Hog

Did you hear about the pigs at a party?

They went whole hog and hog wild.

If you make hamburgers from ground beef, what do you make pork burgers from?

Ground hogs.

One hog said to another, "Stop talking manwash!"

Horse

Once a pony time there lived a coltish lass who wore a ponytail. Although she often said, "Neigh," she never bridled or kicked up her heels at authority. We've herd that she was a real warhorse who champed at the bit to get back in harness each day. Straight from the horse's mouth, that pony was nobody's foal.

Now let's horse around with more wordplay:

As one horse said to another, "I forgot your mane, but your pace is familiar."

Where do newlywed horses stay during their honeymoon?
In the bridle suite.

What goes into the mouth of a quarter horse?
Two bits.

What is a horse's favorite sport?
Stable tennis.

As the horse said as it ate all of its hay, "That's the last straw!"

Hyena

Why did the man cross a parrot and a hyena?
So he could ask what it was laughing about.

Inchworm

What is a drawback of adopting the metric system?
Figuring out what to call the inchworm.

Insect

Did you hear about the dejected bug?
It committed insecticide.

Jaguar

A venerable dame in Nic'raguar
Had her hair nipped off by a jaguar.
The lady gasped, "Ah,"
The jaguar, "Bah,
What a false, artificial old haguar."

Jellyfish

What is a marine policeman's favorite snack?
A jellyfish donut.

Kangaroo

A kangaroo is a pogo stick with a pouch.

What did the mother kangaroo say when she couldn't find her baby?

"Somebody catch that pickpocket!"

What did the kangaroo tell his psychiatrist?

"Why do I always feel so jumpy?"

What is a kangaroo's favorite season?

Spring.

Kid

Announcement on TV: "Attention, goats! It's late at night, and do you know where your kids are?"

Kitten

Why did the cat join the Red Cross?
She wanted to be a first aid kit.

What happened when the poker player's cat swallowed a dime?
There was money in the kitty.

Kiwi

What is the favorite fruit of an Australian flightless bird?
Kiwi.

Koala

What is the favorite drink of Australian bears?
Coca-Koala (a high-koala-T beverage).

Labrador

What did the generous Labrador say when he gave away his bones?

"It is better to give than to retrieve."

Lemming

What did the boy lemming say to the girl lemming?

"I'll follow you to the ends of the earth."

Leopard

Why was the leopard hired by the television news team?
> *To do on-the-spot reports.*

> *There once was a handsome, young shepherd,*
> *Who was eaten at lunch by a leopard.*
> > *Said the leopard, "Egad!*
> > *You'd be tastier, lad,*
> *If you had been salted and peppered."*

Lion

A lion is an animal full of might and mane.

Why did the lion cross the jungle?
> *To get to the other pride.*

Did you hear about the King of the Jungle who won an award for good citizenship?
> *He was a fine and dandy lion.*

Did you hear about the man who was sitting on the steps in front of the New York City Public Library?
> *He was reading between the lions.*

How much do animal trainers in a circus make?
They earn the lion's share of the money.

Why is the King of the Jungle the laziest animal?
Because he's always lion down on the job.

Llama

What do you call a cart used by the chief Tibetan monk to carry around a large, wooly South American animal?
The Dalai Lama's llama dolly.

Lobster

What did the lobster say when placed in a boiling pot?
"Am I in hot water!"

Loon

Did you hear about the crazy birdwatcher?
He was a raven loonatic.

Lox

Did you hear about the deli owner who named an entree after the birds that flew over the Panama Canal?
He called it locks and bay gulls.

Mare

Did you hear about the horse that kept late hours?
It was a nightmare.

Mockingbird

What happened to the mockingbird that swallowed a watch?
She became a tick-tocking bird.

Mole

As the male mole said to his mate, "I worship the ground you tunnel under."

Monkey

What do you get if you run over a monkey?
> *Rhesus pieces.*

How did the chimpanzee escape from its cage?
> *He used a monkey wrench.*

Moose

What has antlers and eats cheese?
> *Mickey Moose.*

Mosquito

Why was the mosquito limping?
> *It flew through a screen door and strained itself.*

Moth

Who spends the summer in a fur coat and the winter in a woolen bathing suit?
> *A moth.*

How do scale-winged insects communicate?
> *By word of moth.*

Mouse

Why did the mouse take a bath?
Because he wanted to be squeaky clean.

How is Mickey Mouse like a comet?
He's a star with a tail.

Why did Mickey Mouse go on a rocket to outer space?
He wanted to find Pluto.

Did you hear about the cat doctor who made mouse calls?

Hickory, dickory, dock,
Some mice ran up the clock.
The clock struck one,
And the rest escaped with minor injuries.

Where did the mouse moor his sailboat?
At the hickory dickory dock.

If you build a better mousetrap, you will catch better mice.

Mule

Did you hear the joke about the mule?
You'll get a real kick out of it.

Mussel

There was a strong man named Russell,
Who liked getting into a tussle.
But he once lost face
At a seafood place,
When he struggled to open a mussel.

Nag

As one horse said to another, "Don't be a nag."

Newt

The salamander was actually a midget lizard, but no one newt.

Octopus

Did you hear about the two octopuses that fell in love?
They walked arm in arm in arm in arm . . . .

Did you hear about the clever marketing manager?
He sold a supply of underarm deodorant to a family of octopuses.

Did you hear about the clumsy octopus that played football?
He still managed to fumble the ball.

Ostrich

A large nine-member family was asleep when a tornado swept through their yard. They were awakened, just as the house was about to collapse, by the squawking of their long-necked pet bird. The headline the next day read: OSTRICH IN TIME SAVES NINE.

Otter

What is the Golden Rule for web-footed mammals?
> *"Do unto otters as you would have them do unto you."*

Owl

Did you hear about the comedian owl?
> *He was a real hoot.*

A wise old owl sat in an oak.
The more he saw the less he spoke.
The less he spoke the more he heard.
Why can't we be like that wise old bird?

Ox

Why did the ox comedian go on strike?
> *Because he couldn't take a yoke.*

Oyster

A noise annoys an oyster.

Did you hear about the angry oyster?
> *It got into a stew.*

Did you hear about the shy oyster?
> *It retreated into its shell and clammed up.*

Parrot

What did the parrot say when it saw a duck?
"Polly wants a quacker."

Did you hear about the parrot that swallowed a watch?
Now it goes tick-talk-tick-talk.

What do you call birds that like to attack ships?
Parrots of the Caribbean.

A parrot made some rude comments to its owner. As punishment, the owner put the parrot in the freezer for several minutes ("to cool its heels," in the owner's words). When the shivering parrot was removed, it pointed inside the freezer and asked its owner, "What did the turkey do to deserve THAT?"

Partridge

Did you hear about the guy who played golf on Christmas and accidentally hit a bird?
He got a partridge on a par three.

Peacock

Why are peacocks unreliable?
They're always spreading tails.

Pelican

Consider the fabulous pelican:
His mouth can hold more than his belican.
He can store in his beak
Enough food for a week.
And it's truly amazing how wellican!

Penguin

Did you hear about the guy who used a computer dating service and requested someone who was short, liked water sports, and wore formal attire?

The computer set him up with a penguin.

Pet

What's furry, barks, and loves school?

A teacher's pet.

Pig

Did you hear about the little girl who grew up with pigs as her pen pals in a rural hamlet?

She wore cute little pigtails and porkpie hats and was happy as a pig in mud when her family carried her around piggyback.

Where do hogs keep their money?

In piggy banks.

What do you call a pig that won the lottery?

Filthy rich.

Stubborn hogs are pigheaded.

Pigeon

Did you hear about the girl who is rather dove-like?
She's not soft and cooing, but she is pigeon-toed.

Pit Bull

A man owned a pit bull who hated to go for walks. The dog kept sitting down and bracing his feet so that his owner would have to drag him by his leash. The owner finally gave up when he realized that he was creating a bottomless pit.

Platypus

As the elephant said to the platypus, "I never forget a face. But with yours I'll make an exception."

Polar Bear

An Alaskan saloon is a polar bar.

Pony

A pony with a sore throat is a hoarse horse.

Poodle

There once was a man with two poodles
Whose first names were Doodles and Toodles.
Their favorite dish
Was not meat or fish.
The poodles loved oodles of noodles.

Porcupine

Show us a porcupine, and we'll show you a thorny issue.

Authorities are seeking a six-foot octopus for the robbery of a convenience store. He is described as "heavily armed." His accomplice is a large porcupine described as "tall, dark, and prickly." Police have issued an "all points" bulletin.

What did the two porcupines say when they kissed each other?
"Ouch!"

What did the porcupine couple name their son?
Spike.

Porpoise

As one dolphin said, after accidentally swimming into another one, "I didn't do it on porpoise."

Prawn

Where can you find good deals on shrimp?
At a prawn shop.

Puffin

Did you hear about the bird that was out of shape?
She was a huffin' puffin.

Puppy

A puppy is a little waggin' without wheels.

Many a dog is adopted because of puppy love.

Quail

What did the cowardly bird do when challenged to a fight?
He quailed at the idea.

Rabbit

What did Bugs Bunny says to the pier?
  "What's up, dock?"

Show us two dozen rabbits in a circle, and we'll show you a 24-carrot ring.

Where do newly married rabbits go?
  On their bunnymoon.

How do bunnies commute to work?
On Rabbit Transit.

Ram

What was the most important animal to the ancient Roman army?
The battering ram.

Rattlesnake

A rattlesnake has a tattle tail.

Raven

Did you hear about the crazy crow?
It was a raven lunatic.

Reindeer

Why did Santa use only seven reindeer last year?

Comet stayed home to clean the sink.

Robin

A robin is a sparrow that spilled ketchup on its chest.

Why was Batman so depressed?
Because Robin flew south for the winter.

Rooster

Sign on a chicken farm: They Roost in Peace.

What does a lazy rooster say?
"Cock-a-doodle-don't."

Sardine

What is the head of a fish school called?
The sar-dean.

Did you hear about the sardines on a subway at rush hour?
They were packed in like commuters.

Seagull

Did you hear about the seabird that landed on a channel marker?

Buoy meets gull.

A pirate returned from war with an eye patch and a wooden arm with a hook, and he was asked by a friend how it happened. "An enemy cannonball hit our mast," explained the pirate, "causing a huge piece of wood to come flying and sever my arm."

The friend then asked, "And are you wearing the eye patch because a splinter from the mast pierced your eye?"

"No," said the pirate, "it was because a seagull deposited a load right smack in my eye."

"You mean," said the friend, "that the seagull's load landed with such force that you lost your eye?"

"No," replied the pirate. "You see, it was the first day that I had my hook."

Seal

Two sea animals were conversing, and one asked, "Can you keep a secret?"

"Yes," replied the other, "my lips are sealed."

What animal is found on every legal document?

A seal.

Sea Lion

Why did the seal get only average grades in school?

Because he was a C-lion.

Seeing Eye Dog

A blind man went into a bookstore, grabbed his seeing-eye dog by the hind legs, and swung the poor pooch back and forth. An astonished salesclerk asked, "May I help you, sir?"

"No, thanks," replied the man. "I'm just browsing."

Setter

Did you hear about the dog who often travels overseas?

He's a jet setter.

Shark

What happened when a shark tried to eat an entire crate of bubble gum?

He bit off more than he could chew.

Did you hear about the underwater billiard player?

He was a pool shark.

What is a shark's favorite game?

Swallow the Feeder.

Sheep

Dogs have fleas, and sheep have fleece.

Sheep farmer No. 1: "Do you know the favorite song of sheep?"

Sheep farmer No. 2: "No. Hum a few baaas."

Did you hear the song about a lamb that has just been sheared?

"Bare, bare back sheep."

Did you hear about Shep Sheep, the comedian?

He was a master of baaad jokes.

In fact, he was a regular knit wit.

Once a heckler called out, "Hey, you got any new jokes?" Shep shot back, "Yes sir, yes sir, three bags full."

His sign-off line was "If I don't see you in the future, I'll see you in the pasture."

Did you hear about the sheep that fell into a vat of chocolate?

He became a Hershey baaa.

Shrimp

How did short Pilgrims arrive in the American colonies?

They came in shrimp boats.

Skunk

A skunk is a community scenter.

Did you hear about the argumentative skunk?

He made a stink everywhere he went.

What happened when a skunk backed into a fan?

It got cut off without a scent.

How many skunks does it take to make a big stink?

Quite a phew.

What's a skunk's favorite game in school?

Show-and-smell.

Slug

A slug is a homeless snail.

Snail

What is the strongest animal?
*The snail, because it carries
its house on its back.*

Where do snails go to eat?
Slow-food restaurants.

A snail bought his first automobile and was so proud of it that he painted a large *S* (for *Snail*) on each side. As he drove along the street, a neighbor exclaimed, "Look at the *S*-car go."

What is another term for the post office?
U.S. Snail Mail.

Snake

How do some snakes communicate with one another?
They make poison-to-poison phone calls.

What did the baby snake say to his mother?
"I hope I'm not poisonous. I just bit my tongue."

Did you hear about the deadly serpent with a lovely singing voice?
It was a choral snake.

Did you hear about the snake trainer who married an undertaker?
They have towels marked "Hiss" and "Hearse."

Sow

How much is the owner of a hundred female pigs and a hundred male deer worth?
Two hundred sows and bucks.

Spaniel

What kind of spaniel likes to draw pictures with its paws?
A cocker doodler.

Spider

Why are spiders like toy tops?
Because they're always spinning.

Why did the fly fly?
Because the spider spied her.

Why did the spider play baseball?
He liked catching flies.

Sponge

What is full of holes but still holds water?
A sponge.

Squid

Why did the octopus go to the psychiatrist?
He was a crazy, mixed-up squid.

Squirrel

Show us a squirrel's home, and we'll show you a nutcracker's suite.

Squirrel No. 1: "I'm just nuts about you."
Squirrel No. 2: "You're nut so bad yourself."

Steer

Said a cow in the pasture, "My dear,
There's not much romance around here.
I start with high hopes
But meet only dopes,
I end up with the usual bum steer."

Stork

Where do herons invest?
In the stork market.

Sturgeon

An artificial fish is a plastic sturgeon.

Swan

What is a bird's economic guideline?
Two can live as cheeply as swan.

Swine

What is a pig's favorite ballet?
Swine Lake.

Swordfish

What was the favorite food of the Three Musketeers?
Swordfish.

Termite

How do termites relax?
By taking a coffee table break.

What did the pet termite eat?
Table scraps.

Tick

What kind of bugs live in clocks?
Ticks.

What arachnid is like the top of a house?
An attick.

Tiger

Why do tigers have stripes?
So they won't be spotted.

Why do leopards have spotted coats?
Because the tigers bought all the striped ones.

Toad

What do you call a dragged cousin of a frog?
A towed toad.

How do amphibians get to the Land of Oz?
They follow the yellow brick toad.

Where do amphibian teachers work?
At toad schools.

Tortoise

Did we tell you about our favorite biology teacher?
She tortoise a real lesson.

Tuna

Did you hear about the fish that knows notes in all scales?
It was a piano tuna.

Turkey

Why did the turkey bolt down his food?
Because he was a gobbler.

Why is a turkey like a ghost?
It's a-gobblin'.

As the mother turkey said to her daughter, who was eating so fast she didn't breathe, "Don't gobble your food."

Turtle

Did you hear about the tortoise with a great memory?
He had turtle recall.

What do you call a tortoise that is an informer?
A turtle-tale.

Why did the turtle cross the road?
To get to the Shell station.

Unicorn

It is risky business to play leapfrog with a unicorn.

Vampire

Dracula can be a real pain in the neck; he can get under your skin and drive you batty.

Why did the vampires stay up all night?
They were studying for their blood tests.

Did you hear about the vampire poet?
Things went from bat to verse.

What do vampires take for a sore throat?
Coffin drops.

Did you hear about the vampire in jail?
He was in a blood cell.

Who does Dracula get letters from?
His fang club.

Vulture

What kind of luggage do vultures take on airplanes?
Carrion.

Did you hear about the vultures who formed a club?
They wanted to go on scavenger hunts.

Wallaby

As one kangaroo said to another, "Wallaby a monkey's uncle!"

Walrus

What do you call a large seal in a hurry?
A walrush.

Wasp

Where do sick hornets go?
   To the waspital.

Weasel

What is the favorite song of certain small, long-tailed mammals?
   "Weasel While You Work."

Weevil

What insect can leap over fourteen cans of bug spray?
   Weevil Knievel.

Werewolf

What do you get when you cross a werewolf with a clay spinner?

   A hairy potter.

Whale

What is Moby-Dick's favorite meal?
   Fish and ships.

What do the British call Moby-Dick?
   The Prince of Whales.

What's at the end of Moby-Dick?
   A whale of a tail.

Wolf

Did you hear about the wolf comedian?
He had his audience howling with laughter.

Woodchuck

*How much wood would a woodchuck chuck
If a woodchuck could chuck wood?
A woodchuck would chuck
All the wood that a woodchuck could chuck
If a woodchuck would chuck wood.*

Woodpecker

A woodpecker in the woods took a powerful peck at the trunk of a huge oak tree. At the very same instant, a bolt of lightning struck and felled the tree. The amazed woodpecker commented to himself, "Wow! I didn't realize my own strength!"

Worm

When we think of caterpillars, we get a worm fuzzy feeling.

Two worms met coming out of their holes in the ground.
"I think I'm in love with you," gushed the first.
"Don't be ridiculous," replied the second. "I'm your other end."

Did you hear about the two silkworms that were in a race?
Neither won because they ended up in a tie.

Wren

A woman tried to thaw out a nearly frozen bird one winter with her hair dryer. Fearful that the bird might not survive, she commented to her husband, "I really shouldn't do this in front of the chilled wren."

Xiphiidae

There's a little-known animal that begins with the letter **X**. It's actually a Greek swordfish, spelled x-i-p-h-i-i-d-a-e, and it's pronounced "ziff-EYE-ih-dee." With that in mind, let's take an alphabetical safari of animals A-Z.

Aardvark a million miles to put 26 animal puns in alphabetical order. I'd **badger** you, and I'd keep **carp**ing on the subject, until I had no **ideers** left. I'd have no **egrets**, however, as I **ferret**ed out more animal puns. If necessary, I'd even **gopher** broke. Some may say it would be a **hare**-brained attempt, but, **iguana** tell you, I'm no **jackass**—and I **kid** you not. I'm not doing this for a **lark** (although maybe just a **mite**). So don't **nag** me. In fact, you **otter** try to **parrot** me. But don't **quail** from the challenge. No one will accuse you of **robin** a bank. Don't be **shellfish**. Avoid taking a **tern** for the worse. Don't be afraid of people saying to you, "**unicorn**iest person I know." Stop crying and **viper** nose. Then say, "**wallaby** a son-of-a-gun" and start singing, "Zip-a-dee doo-dah, **xiphiidae**-ay." Soon you'll be a **yak**-of-all-trades, and can put all of these animal puns in a book called *Who's Zoo*!

Yak

Did you hear about the talkative Tibetan ox?
He was a yackety-yak.

What's the favorite children's toy in Tibet?
A yak-in-the-box.

Zebra

If the alphabet goes from *A* to *Z*, then what goes from *Z* to *A*?

Zebra.

Speaking of the end of the alphabet reminds us of the woman who always peeked at the ending of suspense novels. Even when she received a dictionary as a gift, she turned to the last page and exclaimed, "Hah! The zebra did it!"

PART 2
EVEN MORE
ANIMAL JOKES

50 Rhyming Animals

Have you ever seen a madder adder, a crass bass, a rare bear, an oafish blowfish, a pudgy budgie, a contrary canary, a fat cat, a slick chick, a jolly collie, a sane crane, a mere deer, a legal eagle, a new ewe, a three-inch finch, a shy fly, a straighter gator, a blue gnu, a vanilla gorilla, a bare hare, a purring herring, a round hound, a smitten kitten, a peewee kiwi, a peppered leopard, a mobster lobster, a pink mink, a whole mole, a bandito mosquito, a cool mule, a sloppy okapi, a foul owl, a sweet parakeet, a big pig, a pale quail, an albino rhino, a green sardine, a better setter, a deep sheep, a limp shrimp, a smug slug, a manual spaniel, a wider spider, a wan swan, a flabby tabby, a quick tick, a fertile turtle, a hyper viper, an evil weevil, a firm worm, or a black yak?

10 Animals In Restaurants

A duck waddles into a restaurant and orders a meal.

"That'll be six dollars," says the waiter.

"Just put it on my bill."

A polar bear orders from the menu, "I'll have a ham . . . and cheese . . . sandwich."

The waiter says, "What's with the big pause?"

Replies the bear, "I don't know. I've always had them."

An anteater is sitting at a restaurant table and says that he'd like a sandwich.

"Okay," says the waiter. "How about a hamburger?"

"No-o-o-o-o-o-o-o-o-o," replies the anteater.

"Then how about a hot dog?"

"No-o-o-o-o-o-o-o-o-o."

"A tuna melt?"

"No-o-o-o-o-o-o-o-o-o."

Finally the waiter gets fed up and says, "Hey, listen, buddy, if you don't mind my asking, why the long no's?"

A dog limps into a restaurant on three legs and snarls, "I'm looking for the man who shot my paw!"

A shrimp walks into a soda shop, and the waiter says, "I'm sorry, but we don't serve food here."

Another shrimp walks into a restaurant, and the waiter says, "I'm sorry, but we don't serve shrimp here."

"That's all right," replies the shrimp. "I want to order chicken."

A cat walks into a restaurant and asks the waiter, "Do you serve crabs?"

"Yes," replies the waiter. "We serve everyone."

A man with an alligator walks into a restaurant and asks the owner, "Do you serve tax agents here?"

"Sure do," the owner replies.

"Good. Bring me a pizza," says the man, "and my gator will have a tax agent."

Sitting at a table in a restaurant, a pony says to her server, "I'd like to order the daily special."

The server says "What? I can't hear you. Speak up!"

"May I please have the daily special?"

"What? You have to speak up!"

"Could I please have the daily special?"

"Now listen, if you don't speak up, I won't serve you."

"I'm sorry, I'm just a little hoarse."

A koala bear walks into a restaurant, sits down, and orders a sandwich. He eats the sandwich, pulls out a water pistol, and squirts the waiter. As the koala stands up to go, the owner shouts, "Hey! Where are you going? You just squirted my waiter, and you didn't pay for your sandwich!"

The koala yells back at the bartender, "Hey, man, I'm a ·koala! Look it up!"

The bartender opens his dictionary and sees the following definition for *koala*: "A tree-dwelling marsupial of Australian origin, characterized by a broad head, large hairy ears, dense gray fur, and sharp claws. Eats shoots and leaves."

10 Classroom Classics

Teacher: "Have you ever hunted bear?"
Student: "No, but I've gone fishing in my shorts."

Teacher: "How did you get stung?"
Student: "By smelling a flowber."
Teacher: "There's no *b* in flower."
Student: "There was in this one."

Student: "My pet bird is dead."
Teacher: "That's too bad. How did it die?"
Student: "Flew—"
Teacher: "Bird flu? That's terrible."
Student: "—in front of a bus."

Teacher: "What are four animals that belong to the cat family?"
Student: "The father cat, the mother cat, and two kittens."

Teacher: "If I give you two rabbits and two more rabbits and then another two, how many rabbits will you have?"
Student: "Seven."
Teacher: "Are you sure that the answer isn't six?"
Student: "It's seven. I already have a rabbit at home."
Teacher: "If there were nine cats in a box and two jumped out, how many would be left?"
Student: "None, if they were copycats."

Teacher: "If apples come from apple trees, where do chickens come from?"
Student: "Pole trees."

Teacher: "Why are cows kept in a pasture?"
Student: "So they'll give pasteurized milk."

Teacher: "Please define *noticeable*."
Student: "To spot a male cow."

Teacher: "Use *defeat*, *deduct*, *defense*, and *detail* in a sentence."
Brooklyn student: "De feet of de duck get under de fence before de tail."

20 Animal Crossings

What do you get when you cross two punsters with a hen?
Two comedians who lay eggs with a lot of bad yolks.

In these days of genetic miracles, you never can tell what you'll end up with when you combine one animal with another animal.

What do you get when you cross . . .

. . . a fish with an elephant?
Swimming trunks.

. . . an owl with a goat?
A hootenanny.

. . . a bee with a firefly?
A busy insect that will work all night.

. . . an amoeba with a bunny?
A rabbit that can multiply and divide itself.

. . . an electric eel with a sponge?
A shock absorber.

. . . a rabbit with a spider?
A hare net.

. . . a porcupine with a sheep?
An animal that knits its own sweaters.

. . . a bat with a mole?
A blind date.

. . . a dinosaur with a pig?
Jurassic Pork.

. . . a kangaroo with an elephant?
Potholes all over Australia.

. . . a porcupine with a baby goat?
One stuck-up kid.

. . . a shellfish with a sheep?
A clam chop.

. . . an elephant with an alligator?
An elevator.

. . . an elephant with a rhinocerus?
Elephino!

. . . a centipede with a parrot?
A walkie-talkie.

. . . a skunk with a porcupine?
A pretty lonesome animal.

. . . a dog with a turtle?
An animal that brings you yesterday's newspaper.

. . . a tortoise with a sheep?
A turtleneck sweater.

. . . an octopus with a cat with a centipede?
An animal with eight arms, nine lives, and 100 legs.

. . . a lion with an ocelot?
A lialot, an animal closely related to the cheetalot.

15 Animal Contrasts—Cats and Dogs

What's the difference between racing dogs on a hot day and the authors of this book?

> *The dogs run and pant, while the authors of this book pun and rant.*

And what's the difference between . . .

. . . a cat and a comma?

> *A cat has claws at the end of its paws, and a comma is a pause at the end of a clause.*

. . . a frog and a cat?

> *A frog croaks all the time, a cat only nine times.*

. . . a cat and a match?

> *One is light on its feet, and the other lights on its head.*

. . . a hairy dog and a painter?

> *One sheds his coat, and the other coats his shed.*

. . . a well-dressed man and a tired dog?

> *The man wears a suit, and the dog just pants,*

. . . a missing canine and an exclamation?

> *One is a dog gone, and the other is "doggone!"*

. . . a tough little dog and a small cute minnow?

> *One's a gritty puppy, and the other's a pretty guppy.*

. . . a puppy for sale and one at home?

> *In the pet shop, you choose the pup. At home, it's the pup that chews.*

. . . a mean French dog and a piece of linguine?

One's a nasty poodle, and the other's a pasta noodle.

. . . a neighborhood greeting vehicle and a dog greeting you at the door?

One is a welcome wagon, and the other is a welcome waggin'.

. . . a happy dog and a marine biologist?

One wags a tail, and the other tags a whale.

. . . a barn and a fast dog?

One is a hay ground, and the other a greyhound.

. . . a good dog and a poor student?

One rarely bites, and the other barely writes.

. . . a high-class dog and one that never argues?

One has pedigrees, and the other pet agrees.

. . . a flea-infested dog and a bored houseguest?

One is going to itch, and the other is itching to go.

30 Daffynitions

Somebody once defined *forfeit* as "what many animals stand on." Such "daffynitions" take a fresh approach to the sounds of familiar words, and some of the daffiest can be found in the animal kingdom:

Annoyance: What diluted bug spray does.

Asset: A small donkey.

Bassinet: What a fisherman wants.

Bird of Prey: A religious eagle.

Bulldozer: A sleeping steer.

Cat: A beast of birdin'.

Catnap: To steal a feline.

Coward: A group of cows.

Debate: What you use to catch de fish.

Dogma: A puppy's mother.

Eggplant: Where hens lay.

Fly ball: A dance for bugs.

Gatorade: Help for alligators.

Goblet: A baby turkey.

Hamster: A gangster pig.

Illegal: A sick bird.

Insurmountable: A horse that refuses to be ridden.

Laughing stock: Cattle with a sense of humor.

Mermaid: A deep-she fish.

Microwave: What an amoeba surfs on.

Mutilate: What cats do at night.

Nightmare: A dark horse.

Palomino: A friendly Italian horse.

Polarize: What penguins and walruses see with.

Polecat: A feline from Warsaw.

Pursuit: The cat's pajamas.

Rampage: A call for a male sheep.

Saw Horse: The past tense of "seahorse."

Spot Remover: Dog catcher.

Tadpole: Small stick.

10 Knock-Knock Jokes

Knock, knock. *Who's there?* Hair comb. *Hair comb who?* Hair comb a bunch of knock-knock jokes about animals.

Knock, knock.
Who's there?
Aardvark.
Aardvark who?
Aardvark is the key to success.

Knock, knock.
Who's there?
Amoeba.
Amoeba who?
Amoeba dumb, but I'm not crazy.

Knock, knock.
Who's there?
A burden.
A burden who?
A burden the hand is worth two in the bush.

Knock, knock.
Who's there?
Doughnut.
Doughnut who?
Doughnut count your chickens before they're hatched.

Knock, knock.
Who's there?
Gorilla.
Gorilla who?
Gorilla cheese sandwich for me, please.

Knock, knock.
Who's there?
Iguana.
Iguana who?
Iguana finish my homework.

Knock, knock.
Who's there?
Lion.
Lion who?
Lion to your parents will get you in trouble.

Knock, knock.
Who's there?
Marmalade.
Marmalade who?
"Marmalade me," said the baby chick.

Knock, knock.
Who's there?
Panther.
Panther who?
My panther too short.

Knock, knock.
Who's there?
Zombies.
Zombies who?
Zombies make honey, and zombies don't.

Knock, knock. *Who's there?* Orange. *Orange who?* Now orange you glad that you read all these knock-knock jokes?

10 Jokes About Noah's Ark

How did the animals on Noah's ark survive the great flood?
They were pre-paired.

Did all the animals enter Noah's ark in pairs?
No. The worms came in apples.

What creatures weren't on Noah's ark?
Fish.

Why couldn't Noah catch many fish?
He had only two worms.

Why did the snakes on the ark disobey Noah and not "go forth and multiply"?
Because they were adders.

What animals took the most and the least luggage on Noah's ark?
The elephant took his trunk, but the rooster had only his comb.

Why did Noah take four gnus on the ark?
Because he had good gnus and bad gnus.

What did Noah say while boarding the ark?
"Now I've herd everything."

What did the dinosaurs say when they saw the ark leaving from a distance?
"Oh no. We thought we were supposed to board tomorrow!" (So they became extinct.)

Where did Noah store honey?
In the ark-hives.

10 Pieces of Animal Advice

It's a jungle out there, a real zoo. So here's a collection of beastly wisdom that may help you survive in a dog-eat-dog world that depends on survival of the fittest:

Be like a turtle. You'll make progress by coming out of your shell and sticking your neck out.

Speaking of sticking your neck out, be like a giraffe. Reach higher than all the others, and you'll have the best perspective on life. You'll be head and shoulders above the rest of the herd, and everybody will look up to you.

Be like the birds. They have bills, too, but they keep on singing.

Be like a duck. Keep calm and unruffled on the surface, but paddle like crazy underneath.

Be like a beaver. Don't get stumped. Just cut things down to size and build for the future.

Be like a cat. Claw your way to the top. That's what drapes are for.

Be like a dog. Be loyal. Enjoy the wind in your face. Run barefoot, romp, and play daily. Leave yourself breathless at least once a day. And leave your mark on the world.

Be like a chicken. Rule the roost and suck seed.

Be like a horse. Use some horse sense and stable thinking and be able to say "nay."

Be like a lion. Live life with pride and grab the lion's share with might and mane.

Crack Up Even More With:

WILD & WACKY ANIMAL JOKES

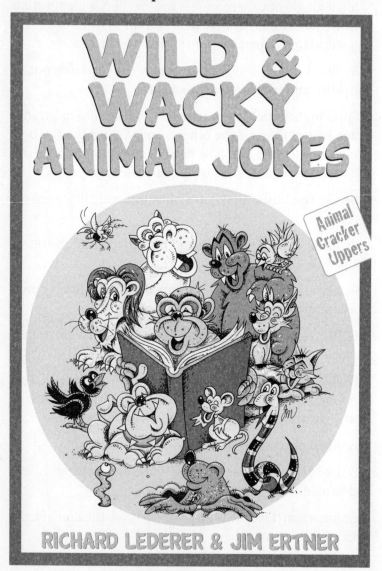

Animal Cracker Uppers

RICHARD LEDERER & JIM ERTNER

IN STORES NOW!